High-Interest READING

by
Walter A. Hazen

Cover Design by
Matthew Van Zomeren

Inside Illustrations by
Don O'Connor

Publisher
Instructional Fair • TS Denison
Grand Rapids, Michigan 49544

Permission to Reproduce

About the Author

Walter A. Hazen received his Bachelor of Science in Education from Troy State University. He also holds a master's degree from the University of Tennessee, where he specialized in deaf education. A secondary history teacher with over 30 years of experience, Walter spent the last several years of his career teaching and developing curriculum for deaf students.

Credits

Author: Walter A. Hazen
Cover Design: Matthew Van Zomeren
Inside Illustrations: Don O'Connor
Project Director/Editor: Sharon Kirkwood
Editors: Lisa Hancock, Eunice Kuiper
Typesetting/Layout: Pat Geasler

Standard Book Number: 1-56822-613-6
High-Interest Reading
Copyright © 1998 by Instructional Fair • TS Denison
2400 Turner NW
Grand Rapids, Michigan 49544

Table of Contents

Answer Key (in middle of book)

Playing for Keeps

Did you ever hear of a game in which every player on the losing team had his heart ripped out and sacrificed to the gods? Talk about the agony of defeat!

Such a game was played by the Mayas and Aztecs in Mexico long ago. The Mayas called the game *ulama*. The Aztecs called it *tlachtli*. By any name, it was not a contest for the timid.

Ulama was similar in some ways to basketball. It was played on a court shaped like the capital letter **I**. The court was sometimes as long as 480 feet, making it 60 yards longer than our football fields. Players had to be in exceptional physical condition to compete in the game.

The object of ulama was to propel a hard rubber ball through a stone disk with a hole in the middle. The disk, which resembled a large doughnut, was attached vertically to a wall 24 feet above the floor of the court.

Compare this with the game of basketball. In basketball, the basket is only 10 feet above the floor and it is attached horizontally to a backboard. The ball is larger and softer and can be touched with the hands.

In ulama, players could not touch the ball with their hands. Some historians maintain that only the hips could be used in advancing the ball. Others say wrists, elbows, and shoulders could be used as well. Whichever was the case, the number of times the ball actually passed through the stone disk was minimal.

Because the rubber ball used in ulama was extremely hard, players wore pads on those parts of the body that came into contact with it. They also wore a type of helmet. Sculptured figurines of ulama players found in Mayan ruins show them outfitted much like modern hockey players.

The winners in ulama were rewarded in a most unusual way. They could claim and keep any items of value worn by the audience in attendance. Sometimes spectators, once they realized the game was nearing its end, tried to sneak out of the stands in order to maintain possession of their valuables. But friends of the winning team usually chased them down and stripped them of their belongings.

Answer the following questions.

1. List two ways in which ulama was similar to basketball.

_____

_____

2. The article points out at least nine differences between ulama and basketball. List five of these on the lines below.

_____

_____

_____

_____

_____

For Discussion

Do you think watching a game of ulama would have been entertaining? Explain.

Indian Princess

There lived in Virginia in the early 1600s a beautiful Indian girl named Pocahontas. Her name meant *Playful One*. She was the daughter of Powhatan, the chief of some 30 Indian tribes in Virginia.

Pocahontas is remembered for saving the life of Captain John Smith. Smith was the leader of the Jamestown colony founded by the English in 1607. In that same year, he was captured by the Indians and sentenced to death by Chief Powhatan. According to Smith's own account, he was ordered to place his head on large stones in anticipation of being clubbed to death by several braves. At this point, Pocahontas is said to have knelt beside the Englishman and placed her head on his. Powhatan was apparently touched by this gesture, and he ordered that Smith be set free.

It is not certain if the above story is true. What casts doubt on its validity is that Smith later claimed to have been saved in the same manner by an Indian girl in New Hampshire.

Regardless, Pocahontas was a real Indian "princess" who did much to improve relations between her people and the English settlers. After the Smith incident, peace prevailed most of the time until Powhatan's death in 1618.

In 1613, Pocahontas was captured and held hostage by the English. During her brief confinement, she converted to

Christianity. She also met and married John Rolfe, a Virginia tobacco planter. In 1616, she accompanied Rolfe to England, where she was presented at the royal court. Pocahontas died there of smallpox in 1617, shortly before her planned return to America. She was buried at Gravesend, England.

John Rolfe returned to Virginia, where he was killed in an Indian uprising in 1622. Thomas, his son by Pocahontas, later became a distinguished Virginian. Today, a number of Virginia families claim to be descendants of Pocahontas and John Rolfe.

Use information from the story about Pocahontas to complete the sentences below.

1. Pocahontas means " _____ One."

2. John Smith was the leader of the Jamestown _____ .

3. Planter John Rolfe grew _____ .

4. Pocahontas died of _____ .

5. _____ was the father of Pocahontas.

6. Pocahontas married John _____ .

7. Pocahontas lived in _____ .

8. Pocahontas saved the life of John _____ .

9. Pocahontas died and was burried in _____ .

10. Thomas Rolfe was the _____ of Pocahontas.

The March of the Lemmings

Scientists spend many hours recording the behavior and habits of animals, searching for clues as to why they act as they do. Through careful observation, the behavior of an animal can usually be explained. But this is not true of the Norwegian lemming of Scandinavia.

Lemmings are rodents that resemble mice. They live in burrows and subsist on a diet of roots and grasses. Every 20–22 days from spring to fall, the females give birth to a litter of up to nine babies. When food is plentiful, lemmings live ordinary lives and attract little attention. But every few years the lemming population explodes, and there are more lemmings than nature can support. When this happens, the lemmings begin an unexplained march to the sea. They do not stop until they plunge to their deaths from cliffs high above the water.

Some people think the lemming migration begins with a huge throng setting out at once. This is not true. The lemmings leave by ones and twos and only form an army when they become backed up by a river or stream. Then their numbers reach the millions as they cross over and continue their journey, eating everything in sight as they move on. Finally, they arrive either at the Atlantic Ocean to the west or at the Gulf of Bothnia to the east. Their long march over at last, they throw themselves into the rough waters of the ocean or the gulf and drown.

Why do lemmings commit mass suicide in this manner?

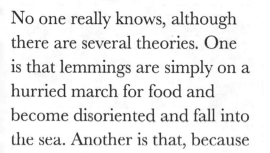

No one really knows, although there are several theories. One is that lemmings are simply on a hurried march for food and become disoriented and fall into the sea. Another is that, because of their increased numbers and the dwindling food supply, they deliberately kill themselves. Perhaps the exact reason for their unusual behavior may never be fully understood.

Place the following sequence of events in the order in which they occurred in the article.

_____ The lemmings reach the ocean or the sea.

_____ The lemmings begin to migrate in ones and twos.

_____ The lemmings form a large congregation when slowed by a natural barrier.

_____ The lemming population increases dramatically.

_____ The lemmings drown by the millions.

Answer the questions below.

1. What part of Europe do the lemmings of this story inhabit?

   _____

2. What do lemmings eat? _____

3. What animals do lemmings resemble? _____

4. Copy one of the sentences in the last paragraph that is an opinion.

   _____

   _____

One-Armed Wonder

During the years the United States was involved in World War II, there was a shortage of quality baseball players in the major leagues. Many of the stars of the game had been drafted into the armed forces and gone off to war. With empty places on most team rosters, players who might otherwise have never made it to the majors had an opportunity to perform at the top level. One such player was Pete Gray.

Gray was born in 1917 in Nanticoke, Pennsylvania. At the age of six, a tragic accident resulted in his right arm being amputated below the elbow. But Pete Gray had a burning desire: he wanted to play baseball, and having just one arm was not going to change his plans. He learned to swing a bat and catch flyballs with his left hand. After much practice, he developed a way to throw a ball after catching it. As quick as a flash,

he would stick his glove under the stump of his right arm, remove the ball with his left hand, and throw back into the infield. His action was slower than normal players but effective enough.

Pete made his high school team and played one year in the outfield. He then quit school to pursue his dream. He played semi-pro ball for a number of years before signing on with a team in the American-Canadian League. In 42 games, he led the league in batting with a .381 average. From 1943 to 1945, he played with the Memphis Chicks of the Southern Association league. He played so well he was voted the league's

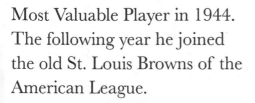

Most Valuable Player in 1944. The following year he joined the old St. Louis Browns of the American League.

Unfortunately, Pete Gray did not enjoy the same success in the majors that he had in the minor leagues. Even with many of the stars going off to war, major league pitching was too fast and hard for the one-armed swinger. In his single season of 1945, he batted only slightly over .200. And his fielding, though miraculous for a person with one arm, was no match for the faster base runners of the major leagues. At the end of the season, the Browns released him, and his playing days all but ended.

But Pete Gray had accomplished what no other person with his handicap had managed: he played in the major leagues.

Indicate by number the order in which the following events in Pete Gray's life occurred.

_____ released by the St. Louis Browns

_____ born in Nanticoke, Pennsylvania

_____ voted the Southern Association's most valuable player in 1944

_____ became a member of the St. Louis Browns

_____ batted just over .200 in 1945

_____ had his right arm amputated following a terrible accident

_____ played for his high school team

_____ led the American-Canadian League in batting

The Flying Congressman

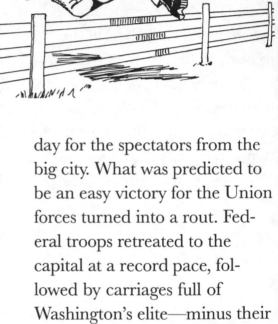

The first major battle of the Civil War was fought near the small town of Manassas Junction, Virginia. The Union army called the battle Bull Run, after the creek by that name. Inasmuch as this quaint little town lay just 30 miles southwest of Washington, D.C., a number of citizens from the nation's capital thought it might be fun to pack a picnic lunch, load up the family, and take a buggy ride out to watch the Confederates "get what was coming to them." They viewed the upcoming battle as nothing more than a sporting event. Even members of Congress were in attendance. No fewer than six Senators and an undetermined number of congressmen showed up, as did pretty ladies in fancy gowns, all traveling in style in expensive buggies and carriages.

One particular congressman provided what turned out to be the only entertainment of the day for the spectators from the big city. What was predicted to be an easy victory for the Union forces turned into a rout. Federal troops retreated to the capital at a record pace, followed by carriages full of Washington's elite—minus their picnic baskets. These were discarded when the rout began, and the Confederate soldiers had a feast when the battle was over.

Although those in flight were preoccupied with their safety, they could not help noticing a tall, long-legged congressman who, on foot, was leading the

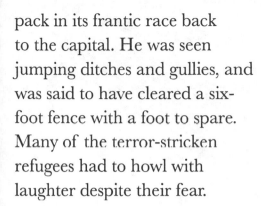

pack in its frantic race back to the capital. He was seen jumping ditches and gullies, and was said to have cleared a six-foot fence with a foot to spare. Many of the terror-stricken refugees had to howl with laughter despite their fear.

History does not relate the name of the fleet and agile congressman. But there is a chance he might be the same legislator who, after reaching the safety of the capital, was confronted by President Lincoln. The President glared at the panting legislator and is supposed to have said dryly, "I congratulate you on winning the race!"

Below are ten **adjectives** taken from the story. On the lines provided, write a synonym and an antonym for each.

	Synonyms	Antonyms
1. major	_____	_____
2. quaint	_____	_____
3. undetermined	_____	_____
4. pretty	_____	_____
5. fancy	_____	_____
6. expensive	_____	_____
7. agile	_____	_____
8. tall	_____	_____
9. frantic	_____	_____
10. fleet	_____	_____

Glass Snakes?

If you live in the Mississippi Valley region or the southeastern part of the United States, you may have at some time come across a glass snake. And you probably jumped just as high as you would have if it had been a real snake.

Glass snakes are not snakes at all. They are one of several kinds of legless lizards that inhabit the earth. Most legless lizards resemble worms, but the glass snake looks very much like a true snake. It gets its name from its ability to break off its fragile tail as easily as a piece of glass. Even though a number of lizards can part with their tails when threatened by an enemy, the glass snake can do it more easily than others. When the tail breaks off from the rest of the lizard's body, it continues to wriggle for a period of time. This allows the lizard to escape while its predator is preoccupied with the wriggling tail.

The glass snake is about two feet long, not including its tail. Its tail is often twice as long as its body. When it sheds its tail, it later grows a new one, although the new tail will be shorter. Glass snakes vary in color from yellow to greenish-brown and sometimes have stripes. Never pick up a glass snake; like a true snake, it inflicts a painful bite.

So, you might ask, if the glass snake is really a lizard, how do snakes and lizards differ? The most obvious difference, of course, is that most lizards have legs, whereas snakes do not. The eyes of lizards can open and close, while those of snakes remain open all the time. Lizards have ears of a sort, while snakes "hear" vibrations through their skull bones. The scales of a lizard's body are pretty much the same size above and below, whereas snakes have a single row of widened scales on their bellies. Finally, as you have learned, many lizards can shed their tails. No snake can do this.

Some people believe that when a lizard breaks off its tail from the rest of its body, the two parts can grow back together again. This is not true. The broken-off tail wriggles for only a short time and then dies.

List five ways in which lizards and snakes are different.

1. _____

2. _____

3. _____

4. _____

5. _____

Rewrite the following sentences to make them true.

1. The tail of a glass snake is one-third as long as its body.

_____

2. Most legless lizards look like snakes.

_____

3. Glass snakes are found throughout the United States.

_____

Danny "Won"duerffel

Some years ago, a highly successful professional football coach attracted attention when he said that "nice guys always finish last." Well, Danny Wuerffel of the University of Florida in Gainesville proved that coach wrong. In 1996, Danny showed the sports world that "nice guys" sometimes do finish first.

Danny Wuerffel was the starting quarterback for the University of Florida football team from 1993 through 1996. Sportswriters delighted in calling him "Danny 'Won'duerffel." And, indeed, his performances on the field were wonderful. In four years as the Gators' quarterback, Wuerffel led his team to four consecutive Southeastern Conference championships. In his senior year, he won the Heisman Trophy, awarded to the nation's best college football player. And on January 2, 1997, he capped his career by leading his Gators to a smashing victory over arch-rival Florida State in the Sugar Bowl. That victory resulted in the University of Florida winning its first-ever national football championship.

Wuerffel, the son of an Air Force chaplain, is an exemplary young man. He neither drinks nor smokes, and he has never been known to use profanity. He is humble and reserved and gives credit for his success to his teammates. On the field, in direct contrast to his coach Steve Spurrier, who occasionally would throw his visor to the ground in frustration, Wuerffel remained calm and collected. By the time he graduated, some of his calmness had begun to rub off on the emotional Spurrier.

How good was Danny Wuerffel during his career at Florida? In four seasons, he completed over 60% of his passes for almost 11,000 yards and 114 touchdowns. Thirty-nine of those touchdown passes came during his super senior year. One can only guess what records he might have set had he not shared quarterbacking duties with a teammate for part of the 1993 and 1994 seasons. Wuerffel finished his career as the most efficient passer in college football history.

The following statements refer to the narrative about Danny Wuerffel. On the line to the left of each sentence, mark **F** if you think the statement is a fact or **O** if you consider it only an opinion.

Danny Wuerffel . . .

_____ 1. is the greatest quarterback ever to play the game.

_____ 2. established records that will never be broken.

_____ 3. led the University of Florida to four straight conference titles.

_____ 4. is admired and respected by all young people.

_____ 5. made the 1996 Gator team the best college football team of all time.

_____ 6. was, in temperament, the direct opposite of his coach, Steve Spurrier.

_____ 7. possesses high personal values.

_____ 8. will be an instant success as a professional quarterback.

Have Legs, Will Run

Pheidippides was a famous runner who lived in Ancient Greece many years ago. In an age long before mail trucks and telephones, runners were important for carrying news and messages from one place to another.

Pheidippides is most remembered for running from Marathon, a coastal plain in Greece, to the city of Athens with news of the Greeks' victory over the Persians. But only days before that historic jaunt, he had completed another run which was much longer. That was a run between the Greek cities of Athens and Sparta.

In 490 B.C., the Greek city-states were threatened by the mighty Persian Empire of King Darius. As the Persian army neared Greece, a small army of Athenians marched out to meet them. At the same time, Athens sent Pheidippides to Sparta to ask for its help. The great runner ran all day and all night to cover the 140 miles between the two cities. When he reached Sparta the following morning, he learned that the Spartans were having a religious festival and would not send any soldiers to assist in the battle. After a brief rest, Pheidippides turned around and ran back to Athens. His journey had covered a combined distance of 280 miles!

But the mighty runner could not enjoy the luxury of a rest. He had to put on his armor and join his fellow soldiers in their fight against the Persians. The two armies met at Marathon, some 25 miles from Athens. Surprisingly, the small group of

Athenians routed the Persians, who turned and fled in their ships. The Athenian commander, fearful that the citizens of Athens would see the ships and surrender, dispatched a runner to the city with news of their great victory. And you guessed it—that runner was Pheidippides!

Pheidippides removed his armor and set off immediately.

In only a few hours, he reached Athens. History relates that when he entered the city, exhausted to the point of death, he shouted, "Rejoice, we conquer!" He then died on the spot.

Pheidippides' run from Marathon to Athens gave name to the present marathon run. But don't you agree his run from Athens to Sparta and back again was even more astonishing?

Match the proper names to the statements by writing the correct letter in the blank.

_____ 1. A famous runner

_____ 2. City-state that refused to help the Athenians

_____ 3. Where Pheidippides ran to after the Battle of Marathon

_____ 4. Whom the Greeks fought at Marathon

_____ 5. A Persian king

_____ 6. Site of famous battle in 490 B.C.

a. Athens

b. Darius

c. Marathon

d. Pheidippides

e. Sparta

f. Persians

Thinking Cap

Why were runners important in ancient times?

The Comical Little Meerkat

In the semidesert of southern Africa lives an unusual little animal called a meerkat. The name itself means *marsh cat*, but the meerkat is neither native to any wetland, nor is it a cat. It is a member of the mongoose family and grows to the size of a large squirrel. It has long claws that it uses to search for food and to dig its underground burrow. The meerkat eats a variety of insects and plant bulbs, as well as lizards, rodents, small snakes, and birds.

Few animals are more considerate and cooperative than the furry little meerkat. When a mother must leave her babies to hunt for food, one adult member of the clan baby-sits, often for an entire day. When the clan hunts as a group, meerkats take turns at guard duty. Standing ramrod straight on its hind legs, the meerkat on duty scans the sky and horizon for predators such as eagles, jackals, and large snakes. It can remain in this upright position for hours. If an enemy is spotted, the alert sentry sounds a shrill alarm, and its fellow meerkats run for cover.

Meerkats are social creatures who seem to carry togetherness to the extreme. When night comes, an entire clan might tumble into the same burrow, piling on top of each other. In this cozy position, they sleep away the hours of darkness.

When morning comes, the meerkat takes on a comical appearance. As the sun begins to warm the desert floor, the members of the clan come out of the burrow to sunbathe. Supported by their stiff tails, and with their front feet folded across their bodies like arms, they stand straight as boards, warming their bellies in the sun for hours. They look even more comical because of their eyes, which are encircled by large black rims. Each meerkat looks as though it was in a fist fight and came out on the losing end!

Some people in South Africa keep meerkats as pets. They are convenient to have around the house when mice and rats are a problem. Thus, even though they are not members of the cat family, they seem capable of performing some of the same duties expected of working cats.

Place a check (✔) to the left of each statement that is true of the meerkat.

The meerkat . . .

_____ 1. lives in a marsh.

_____ 2. suns itself each morning.

_____ 3. is a member of the cat family.

_____ 4. can stand on its hind legs for hours.

_____ 5. prefers to live and hunt alone.

_____ 6. is found throughout Africa.

_____ 7. will often baby-sit another meerkat's young.

_____ 8. is about the size of a large squirrel.

_____ 9. cannot be tamed.

_____ 10. eats only insects.

The Railroad That Wasn't

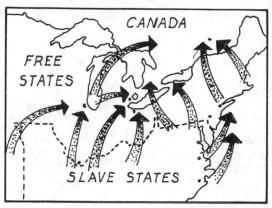

There was once a railroad that was not a railroad at all. Even so, it had conductors, passengers, and stations. And it carried thousands of people to freedom in the years before the Civil War.

Known as the Underground Railroad, it was a system made up of people who helped runaway slaves escape to Canada and to states in the North. It became very important because Congress had passed a series of fugitive slave laws. These laws stated that any slave caught running away could be captured and sent back to his or her owner in the South. Thus, a slave who had escaped to freedom was at great risk of being seized by greedy slave catchers who were paid handsomely for their efforts.

To confuse and avoid the slave catchers, the Underground Railroad used railroad termi-nology in its communications. Slaves who were secretly moved along from place to place were called "passengers," "freight," or "cargo." Houses, barns, and other buildings that hid them by day were known as "stations" or "depots." Those brave people—most of them white—who risked their lives hiding slaves were the "stationmasters." And finally, those men and women who placed their lives in even greater danger by escorting runaway slaves along the various escape routes were called "conductors."

Some conductors were black; others were white. Some were ex-slaves themselves. The most famous was an ex-slave from Maryland named Harriet Tubman. Tubman returned to the South 19 times and helped more than 300 slaves escape to the North. On one trip, she led her brothers and sisters to freedom. On another, she brought out her aging parents. She was so successful that a $40,000 reward was posted for her capture. But Tubman was never caught. She lived out her life in Auburn, New York, opening a home there for needy blacks.

During the years it was in operation, the Underground Railroad was responsible for helping at least 50,000 slaves escape to the North. When the Civil War broke out in 1861, the "railroad," of course, ceased to exist. It was no longer needed.

Identify each of the following terms as they pertained to the Underground Railroad.

1. conductor _____

2. depot _____

3. stationmaster _____

4. cargo _____

Thinking Cap

Pretend you are living in the 1850s. Someone associated with the Underground Railroad requests that you offer your barn as a station along the escape route. What would you do and why?

_____

_____

_____

You Can't Keep a Good Man Down

Most Americans are familiar with the date December 7, 1941. On that bleak day in history, Japanese planes launched from aircraft carriers in the Pacific attacked the U.S. naval base at Pearl Harbor, Hawaii. A complete surprise, the attack came without warning. The Japanese sank or badly damaged 21 ships anchored in the harbor and destroyed more than 300 planes on the ground at nearby airfields. Almost 2,400 American servicemen were killed. More than 1,200 were wounded. In less than two hours, the Japanese had virtually destroyed the U.S. Pacific Fleet, dealing a stunning blow to America's pride.

Many acts of heroism were recorded during those few hours, as Americans fought back in any way they could. On the U.S.S. *Arizona*, a messman who had never fired a gun in his life came up from the ship's kitchen and shot down four enemy planes before his ship sank. At Wheeler Field, a lieutenant and a sergeant standing in the open shot down a low-flying Japanese plane with their rifles. Notable as these incidents were, they were bested by the heroics of a young army pilot named George Bickell.

At the time of the Japanese attack, Lieutenant Bickell was eating breakfast with his wife at their home ten miles from his assigned airfield. As they talked and sipped their coffee, a Japanese plane crashed just outside their home. The young officer and his wife jumped into their car and raced to the airfield. Along the way, they dodged the fire of Japanese planes that were flying very low and shooting at everything in sight.

With his world falling apart around him, Bickell took off in his plane and immediately shot down two enemy aircraft. After returning to Wheeler Field to refuel, he was shot down while attempting to take off again. As his terrified wife watched from a distance, the lieutenant swam 200 yards to shore, got into another plane, took off again, and proceeded to shoot down two more Japanese aircraft. The last one he chased five miles out to sea before bringing it down. The lieutenant had singlehandedly taken on some 20 enemy planes.

Needless to say, Lt. George Bickell received a well-deserved promotion.

Number the events below in the order that they appear in the story.

_____ The Japanese attack on Pearl Harbor begins.

_____ Two servicemen shoot down a Japanese plane with rifles.

_____ Lt. Bickell and his wife hurry to the airfield.

_____ The Bickells have breakfast at home.

_____ Lt. Bickell is promoted to a higher rank.

_____ Lt. Bickell shoots down the first of four enemy planes.

_____ Lt. Bickell swims to shore after being shot down.

_____ A messman on the U.S.S. *Arizona* fires a gun for the first time.

_____ A Japanese plane crashes near the Bickells' home.

_____ Lt. Bickell shoots down his 3rd and 4th Japanese planes.

Doll-Sized Feet

Most little girls spend their days having fun. They laugh, skip, hop, and run about—generally free of all concerns. But the little girls of upper-class China many years ago never knew the luxury of such freedom. For the most part, they sat around crying, dark circles marring their beautiful, little eyes. If they cried too loudly at night so that others in the house could not sleep, their mothers would often beat them with sticks. Sometimes they were even made to sleep outside the main house.

Why were the little girls of China so miserable? It was because of a cruel practice known as footbinding, the purpose of which was to keep their feet forever small and dainty. But the practice left the little girls virtually crippled for life.

First a girl's feet were washed in hot water and massaged. Then the arch of each foot was broken so that the front and back of the foot could be bent to meet. At the same time, the toes of each foot were bent under and pulled toward the heel by a tight, cotton bandage. Each day the bandages were made tighter, causing the young girl no small amount of pain. It was not uncommon—due to the lack of circulation—for the toes to decay and fall off. The end result was that the person could never walk properly. Wherever she went, she toddled along, taking small and painful steps. Sometimes she walked with the aid of a long stick. Sometimes, while still young, she was carried around on a man's back. She simply could not walk on feet that were only three inches in length!

Stories vary as to the origin of footbinding. One concerns a prince whose lady at court had tiny little feet. Wherever she walked, lilies were said to spring from the ground. Thus the reason for calling bound feet "lily feet." The prince was so delighted with his lady's small feet that he ordered the feet of all little girls of the noble class to be bound.

Footbinding began in China in the tenth century and continued for almost a thousand years. In 1912, the last emperor was overthrown, and a democratic government was temporarily set up. Fortunately, this government outlawed the practice of footbinding.

On another sheet of paper, tell why the statements below are false.

1. All little girls in China once had their feet bound.

2. Chinese girls with bound feet were generally happy.

3. Footbinding had no permanent effect on the way a girl walked.

4. Although they were bent and tied under the feet, the toes of girls with bound feet suffered no permanent damage.

5. Chinese mothers openly sympathized with the pain suffered by their footbound daughters.

6. Footbinding was a practice begun after the Communists gained control of China in 1949.

7. Footbinding was a short-lived practice, lasting only several decades.

Captain Stormalong

Just as pioneers, lumberjacks, and others had their heroes, so too did the men who put to sea as a means of livelihood.

Alfred Bulltop Stormalong was a legendary seaman invented by the storytellers of New England. He was a hero of sailors' tall tales during the days of the great sailing ships. Such magnificent vessels ruled the seas until the appearance of the steamship in the late 1800s.

Captain Stormalong was the boatswain, or bosun, on a ship called the *Courser*. His duties included taking charge of the anchor and the riggings. He also supervised the crew in tasks such as loading cargo and maintaining the deck. Even today, navy and merchant marine ships have boatswains who perform similar duties.

The *Courser* was no ordinary ship. It was so huge, so the tale goes, that sailors rode horses on its deck. Its masts were so high that they were made to bend back and forth so the sun and moon could pass. Young sailors who climbed its riggings as boys returned as old men with gray beards.

Stormalong himself was equally imposing. He was as tall as the masts of the ship itself. Some storytellers put his height at four fathoms, or twenty-four feet. He was said to eat ostrich eggs for breakfast and to pick his teeth with an oar. He was so strong and daring that he once tied an octopus' tentacles in knots to free the ship's anchor from its grasp.

At sea, Stormalong could safely guide the *Courser* through

storms that would sink the average ship. Old sailors like to tell of his soaping the sides of the *Courser* so that it could pass through the English Channel. The squeeze was so tight that the soap scraped off on the nearby cliffs. This was how the White Cliffs of Dover were said to have been created.

Fill in the blanks in the sentences below with information from the article.

1. Stormalong was the boatswain, or _____ of a sailing ship.

2. _____ was the middle name of Captain Stormalong.

3. Captain Stormalong's ship was named the _____ .

4. Sailors rode _____ on the *Courser's* deck.

5. Captain Stormalong was a legendary _____ .

6. Storytellers boasted that Stormalong was four _____ in height.

7. Soap scraping off the side of the *Courser* created the White _____ of Dover.

8. Captain Stormalong displayed bad manners by picking his teeth with an _____ .

9. Captain Stormalong once freed the ship's _____ from the tentacles of an octopus.

10. Young sailors who climbed the *Courser's* _____ came down old men with gray beards.

Chomping Cousins

Can you tell the difference between a crocodile and an alligator? Or do you assume, as do some people, that they look pretty much alike?

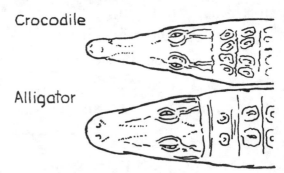

Crocodile

Alligator

Both the crocodile and the alligator belong to a group of reptiles called *crocodilians*. All crocodilians have cigar-shaped bodies and look like giant lizards. All have tough skins made up of hard, bony plates and scales.

Crocodiles and alligators have even more in common than their shape and skin. They have short legs and long, powerful tails that they sweep from side to side when swimming. Both are good swimmers and dine mostly on fish, birds, turtles, snakes, and any small mammals they can catch. Large males of both species have been known to attack larger animals such as dogs and cattle, and even to attack people. Alligators drag their prey underwater until they drown. Then they tear them to pieces. Crocodiles latch onto their prey and twist them into pieces by spinning lengthwise very rapidly in the water.

The best way to tell a crocodile from an alligator is by observing its snout. The snout of the crocodile is narrow and tapers nearly to a point at the tip. The snout of the alligator is broader and rounded at the end. The crocodile is also lighter and quicker than the alligator and much more vicious. It is not unusual for some types of crocodiles to leave the water to attack human beings. The more timid alligator normally will not attack humans unless it is hungry or provoked.

Crocodiles are found on every continent except Europe and Antarctica. Alligators, except for a species native to eastern China, are limited to the Americas. In the United States, they inhabit the swamps, rivers, and coastal areas of several southern states.

Compare and contrast the crocodile and the alligator in the Venn Diagram. Write any similarities where the circles overlap.

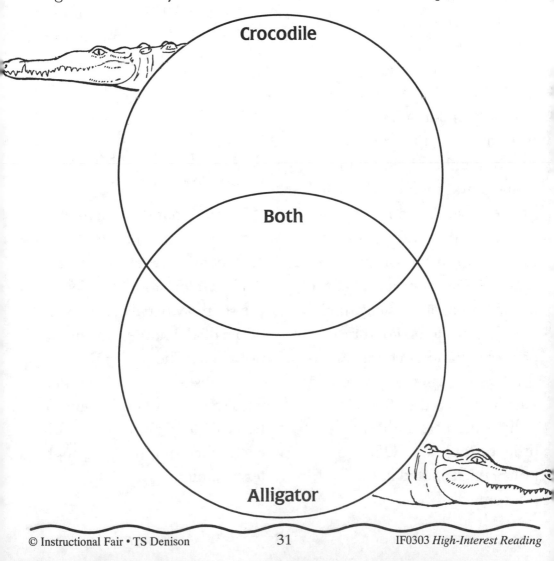

Crocodile

Both

Alligator

Night of Terror

Golda Meir was the prime minister of Israel from 1969 to 1974. She has been one of a handful of women who have headed their country's government.

Golda Meir's life was not always so grand. She was born Golda Mabovitz, to a poor family in Kiev, Ukraine, in 1898. Because she was Jewish, her early childhood memories were mostly unpleasant ones. She remembers being cold, hungry, and frightened much of the time. Russia in the nineteenth century was notorious for its pogroms. Pogroms were planned massacres or killings of innocent people. Usually these people were Jews. Pogroms occurred in other countries, but they were particularly severe in Russia. When they broke out, police and local authorities did little to stop them. Often local police participated in the pogroms.

As a little girl, Golda was too young to understand fully this hatred directed against her people. But she was old enough to know that a pogrom meant her life was in danger. She clearly remembered one terrifying night in 1903 or 1904, when rumors of a planned pogrom spread to her neighborhood. She watched in panic as her father and another man—whose famililies shared a house—boarded up all doors and windows to the two-story apartment house.

Throughout the long night, scores of people passed the house on foot and horseback. All the while, Golda stood terrified on the stairway between the two floors of the house. But she was not alone. The Jewish family living upstairs had a daughter who was about Golda's age. The two frightened little girls held each other, trembling through the terrible night.

Golda and the others in her house were lucky. The pogrom that night did not harm the Mabovitzes or the family upstairs. The shouting mob outside left the house undisturbed. Other families were not so fortunate. Houses were broken into and people were killed.

Golda Mabovitz and her family later emigrated to the United States. In 1921, Golda and her husband went to Palestine (later to become Israel) and joined a kibbutz, a collective farm. She joined an organization struggling to establish a Jewish nation. That struggle became a reality in 1948, when the state of Israel was created. Golda became its prime minister 21 years later.

The meaning of a word often depends on its context, or the way it is used in a sentence. With this in mind, use the words from the word bank to fill in the blanks in the narrative below.

Word Bank				
adult	early	feared	little	unpleasant
cold	family	survived	vividly	differently

As an _____ , Golda Meir could recall _____ of her _____ childhood. But what she did remember was often _____ to talk about.

Golda's _____ was poor. She mostly remembered the years of hunger and _____ . And she very _____ remembered the one night in Kiev when she _____ for her life. Do you think the history of Israel might have turned out _____ if Golda had not _____ that terrible night?

Careless Cow

In the years following the Civil War, Chicago became the railroad and commercial center of America. From a small village of about 150 people in 1833, the town grew so rapidly that by 1870 its population numbered 300,000. With business thriving and times good, no one was prepared for what happened in the evening hours of October 8, 1871.

For nearly a year, the Chicago area had suffered from a severe drought, and the city, with so many wooden buildings, was a tinderbox waiting to ignite. Carelessness on the part of anyone would have set off a disaster. Inevitably, such a disaster did occur. A fire broke out in the lumber district and, with the help of a strong west wind, spread quickly through the city. The fire burned out of control for more than 24 hours. By the time it ended, it had become one of the worst fires in U.S.

history and caused almost $200 million in property damage. One of the few buildings to remain standing was the three-year-old water tower. As many as 90,000 Chicagoans were left homeless. At least 300 people were killed.

Although some sources say that the cause of the fire was never determined, others blame it on a cow—or, rather, on the cow's owner. Supporters of this theory maintain that a Mrs. O'Leary went out to her barn the evening of October 8 to milk her cow. Heedless of the dry conditions, she carried a lighted kerosene lantern into the barn with her. As she got ready to perform her chore, the cow kicked over the lantern and started a fire inside the dry barn. Then, with the help of the wind, plus the dry conditions, the fire soon engulfed the entire city.

The city of Chicago was rebuilt in record time with wider streets and buildings made of stone and steel. By 1890, its population had grown to one million. But still the question remained: Did Mrs. O'Leary's cow start the fire that nearly destroyed one of America's largest cities?

Circle the correct word(s) to complete each statement below.

1. The fire that destroyed Chicago occurred (before, after, during) the Civil War.

2. The fire began in Chicago's (grain, cattle, lumber) district.

3. About (300, 2,124, 17,000) people died in the Chicago fire.

4. The fire left (17, 90, 300) thousand people homeless.

5. Property damage from the fire totaled almost 200 (thousand, million, billion) dollars.

6. The fire burned for more than (a week, a month, a day).

7. The chances of Chicago having a major fire at the time were great because (Chicago's citizens were careless; rain had not fallen for some time; everyone used kerosene lanterns).

8. After the fire, Chicago was rebuilt (slowly, rapidly, in stop-and-go fashion).

Thinking Cap

Is the story about the Chicago fire starting in Mrs. O'Leary's barn and then burning most of the city credible (believable)? Explain.

Up, Up, and Away

You may have heard of Laika, the dog the Russians launched into orbit in November 1957. Laika was the first animal to travel in space.

But Laika was not the first living thing to *fly* in an aircraft. That distinction belongs—not to one—but to three animals. Oddly enough, the animals were a duck, a rooster, and a sheep. Their feat was accomplished in the basket of a hot-air balloon sent aloft in France in 1783.

Two brothers, Jacques and Joseph Montgolfier, had invented the hot-air balloon a few months before the flight of the three animals. They first launched it (empty) on June 4, 1783. It rose to a height of 6,000 feet and thrilled a sizeable crowd at the small French town of Annonay.

The Montgolfiers were more fortunate with their balloon than was one of their competitors, a physicist named Jacques Charles.

With the help of mechanics, Charles built and launched a balloon in August of the same year. But when his balloon landed in the French country-side, terrified peasants attacked it and beat it to pieces.

By September, the Montgolfiers were ready to test their balloon with live occupants. The three animals were thus volunteered for the flight. Taking off at Versailles with the duck, the rooster, and the sheep, the balloon flew for some two miles and stayed aloft for eight minutes. It landed safely, and the animals appeared none the worse for the ordeal.

About two months after the animals' flight, the first humans to go aloft in the Montgolfier brothers' balloon took off from

Answer Key

High-Interest Reading—Grade 5

Page 5

1. Played on a court.
   Player had to "shoot" a ball through a round opening.
2. Some suggested answers:
   - Ulama court was longer.
   - Ulama "basket" was higher.
   - Disk was vertical to the floor.
   - Players could not use their hands.
   - Used a hard, rubber ball.
   - Players wore pads and helmets.

For Discussion: Answers will vary.

Page 7

Use information from the story about Pocahontas to complete the sentences below.

1. Pocahontas means "_Playful_ One."
2. John Smith was the leader of the Jamestown _colony_.
3. Planter John Rolfe grew _tobacco_.
4. Pocahontas died of _smallpox_.
5. _Powhatan_ was the father of Pocahontas.
6. Pocahontas married John _Rolfe_.
7. Pocahontas lived in _Virginia_.
8. Pocahontas saved the life of John _Smith_.
9. Pocahontas died and was buried in _England_.
10. Thomas Rolfe was the _son_ of Pocahontas.

Page 9

Place the following sequence of events in the order in which they occurred in the article.

_4_ The lemmings reach the ocean or the sea.
_2_ The lemmings begin to migrate in ones and twos.
_3_ The lemmings form a large congregation when slowed by a natural barrier.
_1_ The lemming population increases dramatically.
_5_ The lemmings drown by the millions.

Answer the questions below.

1. What part of Europe do the lemmings of this story inhabit?
   Scandinavia
2. What do lemmings eat? _roots and grasses_
3. What animals do lemmings resemble? _mice_
4. Copy one of the sentences in the last paragraph that is an opinion.
   1. ...become disoriented...
   2. ...deliberately kill themselves.

Page 11

Indicate by number the order in which the following events in Pete Gray's life occurred.

_8_ released by the St. Louis Browns
_1_ born in Nanticoke, Pennsylvania
_5_ voted the Southern Association's most valuable player in 1944
_6_ became a member of the St. Louis Browns
_7_ batted just over .200 in 1945
_2_ had his right arm amputated following a terrible accident
_3_ played for his high school team
_4_ led the American-Canadian League in batting

Page 13

Suggested answers:

Below are ten **adjectives** taken from the story. On the lines provided, write a <u>synonym</u> and an <u>antonym</u> for each.

1. major	important	minor
2. quaint	old-fashioned	ordinary
3. undetermined	undecided	known
4. pretty	attractive	plain
5. fancy	ornate	simple
6. expensive	costly	cheap
7. agile	nimble	clumsy
8. tall	high; big	short
9. frantic	frenzied	calm
10. fleet	fast	slow

Page 15

List five ways in which lizards and snakes are different.

1. Most lizards have legs; snakes do not.
2. Lizards' eyes open and shut.
3. " have ears; snakes: vibrations through skull.
4. Their scales are different.
5. Lizards can shed their tails; snakes cannot.

Rewrite the following sentences to make them true.

1. The tail of a glass snake is one-third as long as its body.

... is twice as long ...

2. Most legless lizards look like snakes.

... look like worms.

3. Glass snakes are found throughout the United States.

... in southeastern U.S. and Mississippi Valley.

Page 17

The following statements refer to the narrative about Danny Wuerffel. On the line to the left of each sentence, mark **F** if you think the statement is a fact or **O** if you consider it only an opinion.

Danny Wuerffel . . .

- **O** 1. is the greatest quarterback ever to play the game.
- **O** 2. established records that will never be broken.
- **F** 3. led the University of Florida to four straight conference titles.
- **O** 4. is admired and respected by all young people.
- **O** 5. made the 1996 Gator team the best college football team of all time.
- **F** 6. was, in temperament, the direct opposite of his coach, Steve Spurrier.
- **F** 7. possesses high personal values.
- **O** 8. will be an instant success as a professional quarterback.

Page 19

Match the proper names to the statements by writing the correct letter in the blank.

- **D** 1. A famous runner
- **E** 2. City-state that refused to help the Athenians
- **A** 3. Where Pheidippides ran to after the Battle of Marathon
- **F** 4. Whom the Greeks fought at Marathon
- **B** 5. A Persian king
- **C** 6. Site of famous battle in 490 B.C.

a. Athens
b. Darius
c. Marathon
d. Pheidippides
e. Sparta
f. Persians

Thinking Cap Suggested answer.

Why were runners important in ancient times?
Carried news and messages.

Page 21

Place a check (✔) to the left of each
statement that is true of the meerkat.

The meerkat . . .

_____ 1. lives in a marsh.

__✔__ 2. suns itself each morning.

_____ 3. is a member of the cat family.

__✔__ 4. can stand on its hind legs for hours.

_____ 5. prefers to live and hunt alone.

_____ 6. is found throughout Africa.

__✔__ 7. will often baby-sit another meerkat's young.

__✔__ 8. is about the size of a large squirrel.

_____ 9. cannot be tamed.

_____ 10. eats only insects.

Page 23

Identify each of the following terms as they pertained to the
Underground Railroad.

1. conductor *led slaves to freedom;*

2. depot *hiding place during the day*

3. stationmaster *person who hid runaways*

4. cargo *slaves who were moving from place to place*

Thinking Cap

Pretend you are living in the 1850s. Someone associated with the
Underground Railroad requests that you offer your barn as a station
along the escape route. What would you do and why?

Answers will vary.

_____

_____

Page 25

Number the events below in the order that they appear in the story.

_1_ The Japanese attack on Pearl Harbor begins.

_3_ Two servicemen shoot down a Japanese plane with rifles.

_6_ Lt. Bickell and his wife hurry to the airfield.

_4_ The Bickells have breakfast at home.

_10_ Lt. Bickell is promoted to a higher rank.

_7_ Lt. Bickell shoots down the first of four enemy planes.

_8_ Lt. Bickell swims to shore after being shot down.

_2_ A messman on the U.S.S. *Arizona* fires a gun for the first time.

_5_ A Japanese plane crashes near the Bickells' home.

_9_ Lt. Bickell shoots down his 3rd and 4th Japanese planes.

Page 27

On another sheet of paper, tell why the statements below are false.
Suggested answers:

1. All little girls in China once had their feet bound.
... Only girls of the upper class

2. Chinese girls with bound feet were generally happy.
... usually in a lot of pain.

3. Footbinding had no permanent effect on the way a girl walked.
... crippled girls for life.

4. Although they were bent and tied under the feet, the toes of
girls with bound feet suffered no permanent damage.
... often, toes decayed + fell off.

5. Chinese mothers openly sympathized with the pain suffered by
their footbound daughters.
... often, beat daughters for crying.

6. Footbinding was a practice begun after the Communists gained
control of China in 1949. *... began in the 10ᵗʰ century*

7. Footbinding was a short-lived practice, lasting only several
decades. *... lasted almost 1000 years.*

Page 29

Fill in the blanks in the sentences below with information from the article.

1. Stormalong was the boatswain, or **bosun** of a sailing ship.
2. **Bulltop** was the middle name of Captain Stormalong.
3. Captain Stormalong's ship was named the **Courser**.
4. Sailors rode **horses** on the *Courser's* deck.
5. Captain Stormalong was a legendary **seaman**.
6. Storytellers boasted that Stormalong was four **fathoms** in height.
7. Soap scraping off the side of the *Courser* created the White **Cliffs** of Dover.
8. Captain Stormalong displayed bad manners by picking his teeth with an **oar**.
9. Captain Stormalong once freed the ship's **anchor** from the tentacles of an octopus.
10. Young sailors who climbed the *Courser's* **riggings** came down old men with gray beards.

Page 31

Crocodile
1. snout: narrow and pointed
2. lighter, quicker, and more vicious
3. found on every continent except Europe and Antarctica

Alligator
1. snout: broad and rounded
2. more timid
3. limited primarily to the Americas

Both
1. belong to same group
2. cigar-shaped bodies
3. look like lizards
4. skin of bony plates and scales
5. short legs
6. powerful tails
7. good swimmers
8. eat fish, birds, any animals

Page 33

The meaning of a word often depends on its context, or the way it is used in a sentence. With this in mind, use the words from the word bank to fill in the blanks in the narrative below.

Word Bank				
adult	early	feared	little	unpleasant
cold	family	survived	vividly	differently

As an **adult**, Gold Meir could recall **little** of her **early** childhood. But what she did remember was often **unpleasant** to talk about.

Golda's **family** was poor. She mostly remembered the years of hunger and **cold**. And she very **vividly** remembered the one night in Kiev when she **feared** for her life. Do you think the history of Israel might have turned out **differently** if Golda had not **survived** that terrible night?

Page 35

Circle the correct word(s) to complete each statement below.

1. The fire that destroyed Chicago occurred (before, (after,) during) the Civil War.
2. The fire began in Chicago's (grain, cattle, (lumber)) district.
3. About ((300,) 2,124, 17,000) people died in the Chicago fire.
4. The fire left (17, (90,) 300) thousand people homeless.
5. Property damage from the fire totaled almost 200 (thousand, (million,) billion) dollars.
6. The fire burned for more than (one week, a month, (a day)).
7. The chances of Chicago having a major fire at the time were great because ((Chicago's citizens were careless; (rain had not fallen for some time)) everyone used kerosene lanterns).
8. After the fire, Chicago was rebuilt (slowly, (rapidly,) in stop-and-go fashion).

Thinking Cap *Answers will vary.*
Is the story about the Chicago fire starting in Mrs. O'Leary's barn and then burning most of the city credible (believable)? Explain.

Page 37

Identify the following from the article.

1. Jacques and Joseph Montgolfier *brothers, who made first hot-air balloon*
2. Laika *dog Russians launched into orbit*
3. Annonay *small town in France*
4. Jacques Charles *French physicist who built and launched a balloon*
5. Pilâtre de Rozier and the Marquis d'Arlandes *first humans to go aloft in balloon*
6. Versailles *city where animals flew in balloon*

Write a synonym for each of these words from the story:

1. sizeable *large*
2. launched *send forth*
3. aloft *in the air*
4. fortunate *lucky*
5. worse *less favorable*
6. narrowly *barely*

Page 39

Use the Word Bank to fill in the blanks in the sentences below.

Word Bank		
black	failed	sycamore
burning	fastened	sympathized
cold	saved	transport

1. In the beginning, all the animals were very *cold*.
2. The gods of thunder *sympathized* with the plight of the animals.
3. The gods of thunder made a lightning bolt strike a *sycamore* tree.
4. The *burning* tree delighted the animals.
5. The animals discussed ways to *transport* the fire from the island to the mainland.
6. Both the Raven and the Racer Snake are *black* because of their efforts to transport the fire.
7. Several owls also *failed* to accomplish the task.
8. The Water Spider *saved* the day for the animals.
9. The Water Spider carried a hot coal to the mainland in a small bowl it had woven and *fastened* to its back.

Page 41

Cold:
1. slight fever
2. can occur almost anytime
3. sore throat; runny nose

Flu:
1. more serious
2. can have high fever
3. headache and muscles ache
4. related to epidemics
5. nausea, vomiting; dry cough

Both:
1. caused by viruses
2. transmitted by sneezing and coughing
3. lasts a few days to a week and a half
4. can lead to bronchitis and pneumonia

Page 43

Number the following events in the life of Bill Pickett in the order that they occured.

Bill Pickett . . .

3 joined a wild west show.
5 bought a large ranch in Oklahoma.
1 became a cowboy.
4 took on a bull in a Mexico City bull ring.
2 invented or started bulldogging.

Thinking Cap
Answers will vary—may have been motivated because he was black

Page 45

Write the letter of the correct answer that completes each statement.

c 1. Cumberland agreed to a game with Tech because . . .
   a. the players thought it would be a lot of fun.
   b. Cumberland's coach thought his team had a good chance at winning.
   c. the college was offered a sum of money to play.

b 2. Cumberland's strategy of kicking off rather than receiving after each Tech score was an attempt to . . .
   a. improve on its kicking game.
   b. hold the score down.
   c. confuse the Tech team.

a 3. Georgia Tech scored an equal number of points in the . . .
   a. first and second quarters.
   b. first and third quarters.
   c. second and fourth quarters.

b 4. The game was played in . . .
   a. Lebanon, Tennessee.
   b. Atlanta, Georgia
   c. a site not revealed by the story.

Page 47

Answer the following questions:

1. How did the armadillo get its name? *from Spanish word that means "little armored thing"*

2. What makes it possible for an armadillo to roll its shell into a ball? *shell consists of overlapping plates*

3. What do armadillos eat? *roots, insects, worms, fruits*

4. Where is the armadillo found in the United States? *in south-central and southeastern U.S.*

5. What is unusual about the babies born to a female armadillo? *They are all always the same sex.*

6. How is the armadillo able to float? *Swallowed air turns shell into a boat.*

7. Why is the armadillo sometimes eaten as a delicacy? *Its flesh has a pork-like taste.*

Page 49

Place a check (✓) in the blank to the left of each statement that is **true** of Molly Pitcher.

_____ 1. My real name was Margaret Corbin.

✓ 2. I was married to a soldier.

✓ 3. I followed my husband to camp and into battle.

✓ 4. I am a heroine of the Revolutionary War.

_____ 5. I fought at Fort Washington.

_____ 6. My husband was overcome by heat at the Battle of Monmouth.

✓ 7. I took over and fired my husband's gun.

✓ 8. I carried pitchers of water to soldiers at Monmouth.

✓ 9. I was granted a pension by the state of Pennsylvania.

_____ 10. A monument at West Point was dedicated in my honor.

_____ 11. I was given an officer's commission by George Washington.

_____ 12. I was wounded at the Battle of Monmouth.

Page 51

The meaning of a word sometimes depends on the way it is used in a sentence. Use the Word Bank to fill in the blanks below.

The tank was *introduced* to the battlefield by the British in Word War I. When it *appeared* at the Somme in 1916, it *terrified* the Germans.

An earlier tank used by the British *proved* ineffective. It got *stuck* in ditches and had a *tendency* to overturn. Its *successor*, called Big Willie, was *more* reliable. And it could *attain* a speed of almost 4 mph!

Big Willie was a *cumbersome* machine that *resembled* a big, metal box. But it *fulfilled* its purpose. When the Germans first saw it, they *gazed* in amazement. Many thought the *monstrosity* was funny. Then it began to *belch* fire. At that, the Germans turned and fled.

		Word Bank		
appeared	cumbersome	introduced	proved	resembled
attain	fulfilled	monstrosity	stuck	tendency
belch	gazed	more	successor	terrified

Page 53

Write the letter of the correct answer to each statement.

_c_ 1. The duckbill platypus is native only to . . .
    a. Tasmania.
    b. Australia.
    c. both of the above.

_a_ 2. Poisonous spurs are located on the hind legs of the . . .
    a. male platypus.
    b. female platypus.
    c. both.

_b_ 3. The female platypus lays . . .
    a. only one egg at a time.
    b. no more than two to three eggs at a time.
    c. up to five eggs at a time.

_c_ 4. When a platypus moves around, it resembles a (an) . . .
    a. badger.
    b. duck.
    c. alligator.

_a_ 5. The diet of the platypus consists of . . .
    a. worms, grubs, and shellfish.
    b. fruits and berries.
    c. small rodents.

Page 55

Number the events below about Pecos Bill in the order that they appear in the story.

Pecos Bill . . .

_7_ became boss of a trail outfit.
_2_ fell near the Pecos River.
_6_ tamed a mountain lion and a rattlesnake.
_1_ bounced off a wagon while on his way west.
_4_ dug the Rio Grande River.
_3_ grew up with coyotes.
_5_ took a ride on a cyclone.

Write meanings for the following words from the story. You may use a dictionary if necessary. _Suggested answers:_

1. fearsome _causing fear_
2. drought _long period of dry weather_
3. cyclone _violent windstorm—tornado_
4. destination _place to which one travels_
5. exploits _deeds; bold unusual acts_

Page 57
Answers will vary.

Page 59
Using words from the story, fill in the blanks in the sentences below to complete the puzzle about Tom Thumb.

1. Tom Thumb weighed _15_ pounds as a young boy.
2. Charles _Stratton_ was Tom Thumb's real name.
3. In size, Tom Thumb was a _midget_.
4. Tom was a performer with *The Greatest Show on* _Earth_.
5. The Feejee Mermaid was a _hoax_.
6. Tom Thumb toured _Europe_ on several occasions.
7. Phineas T. _Barnum_ was Tom Thumb's employer.
8. The "Prince of _Humbug_" probably fooled many people in his lifetime.

Thinking Cap _Possible answer:_
Why do you think Charles Stratton's parents allowed him to join Phineas T. Barnum's museum at the tender age of four?
Probably for money.

Page 61

Match the year to the event by writing the correct letter in the blank to the left of each statement.

    A. 1883   C. 1873
    B. 1890   D. 1882

_A_ 1. year by which most of the buffalo had disappeared.
_D_ 2. year in which only about 540 buffalo remained in the United States.
_C_ 3. year 1,250,000 hides were shipped east.
_B_ 4. year in which resistance on the part of the Plains Indians ended.

Thinking Cap _Suggested answer:_
Explain the position of the government toward the slaughter of the buffalo. _Government saw buffalo's destruction as a way to subdue the Indians._

Page 63

On the blank line to the left of each sentence, write **T** if the statement is true or **F** if it is false.

_F_ 1. Marsupials live only on the ground.

_T_ 2. The koala's diet consists solely of the leaves of the eucalyptus tree.

_T_ 3. The largest marsupial is the red kangaroo.

_F_ 4. The Tasmanian devil subsists chiefly on a diet of insects.

_F_ 5. The wallaby is a kind of wolf.

_T_ 6. Most marsupials live in Australia.

_F_ 7. The Tasmanian wolf has increased in numbers so much that it is a threat to farmers.

_F_ 8. The koala is a true bear.

_T_ 9. Red kangaroos stand as tall as most men.

_F_ 10. The opossum is the smallest of the marsupials.

Page 65

Write the letter of the correct answer in the blank to the left of each question.

_a_ 1. Rock's first superstar was . . .
  a. Elvis Presley.
  b. Bill Haley.
  c. Bruce Springsteen.

_c_ 2. Near the end of the 1950s, rock 'n' roll . . .
  a. became more popular than ever.
  b. spread internationally.
  c. experienced a temporary decline.

_b_ 3. The first important rock band of the 1950s was . . .
  a. the Jefferson Airplane.
  b. Bill Haley and the Comets.
  c. the Rolling Stones.

_c_ 4. The following is true of rock 'n' roll music of the 1950s
  a. Young people claimed it as their own.
  b. It was simple, with easy melodies and just a few chords.
  c. Both "a" and "b" are true.

_c_ 5. The song "Maybellene" was recorded by . . .
  a. Elvis Presley.
  b. Madonna.
  c. Chuck Berry.

_a_ 6. The first big international rock group was . . .
  a. the Beatles.
  b. the Rolling Stones.
  c. the Bee Gees.

Page 67

The following statements refer to the story of Mike Fink. On the line to the left of each sentence, mark **F** if you think the statement is a fact, or **O** if you consider it an opinion.

_O_ 1. Mike Fink was the strongest man on the frontier.

_F_ 2. Mike Fink moved west when the steamboat came into use.

_O_ 3. Everybody on the frontier respected Mike Fink.

_O_ 4. Mrs. Peg Fink was afraid of her husband.

_F_ 5. Mike Fink liked to brag and fight.

_O_ 6. Carpenter's friend was justified in killing Mike Fink.

_F_ 7. Stories such as that of Mike Fink tell us much about early frontier people.

_F_ 8. Mike Fink is not a good role model for young people to follow.

_O_ 9. Fighting and the telling of tall tales were characteristic of frontier people.

Draw a sketch. Find a picture of a keelboat in an encyclopedia or some other source and draw a sketch of it on another sheet of paper.

Page 69
Answers will vary.

Page 71

Parts of Speech		Synonyms
verb	1. destined	fated
adjective	2. superior	better
noun	3. endeavor	undertakings
adjective	4. far-fetched	illogical
verb	5. brood	mope
noun	6. edge	advantage
verb	7. shatter	destroy
noun	8. parade	motorcade
verb	9. outshine	upstage
verb	10. conquered	overran

Word Bank			
advantage	motorcade	undertaking	illogical
fated	better	destroy	upstage
	overrun	mope	

a site outside Paris. The two occupants, Pilâtre de Rozier and the Marquis d'Arlandes, drifted for about 25 minutes. Their adventure quickly turned into a comedy of errors. The fabric of which the balloon was made caught fire and the men spent the better part of their time trying to put it out with wet sponges. They also came close to scraping rooftops along the way, and narrowly missed hitting two windmills. But they landed safely some five miles from where they had started and wrote their names in the history books.

Identify the following from the article.

1. Jacques and Joseph Montgolfier _____

   _____

2. Laika _____

3. Annonay _____

4. Jacques Charles _____

   _____

5. Pilâtre de Rozier and the Marquis d'Arlandes _____

   _____

6. Versailles _____

Write a synonym for each of the following words from the story:

1. sizeable _____   4. fortunate _____

2. launched _____   5. worse _____

3. aloft _____   6. narrowly _____

How the Animals Got Fire

Of all the stories invented by Native Americans to explain nature and the surrounding world, none is more charming than the Cherokee legend about how fire came to the earth.

The Cherokees believed that early humans and animals inhabiting the earth were cold! Even with their fur and feathers, the animals were still cold. After some time, the gods of thunder, feeling sorry for them, sent a bolt of lightning to strike a hollow sycamore tree on a small island. The animals were amazed and delighted with the warmth provided by the burning tree, but one problem remained. How were they to transport the fire from the island to the mainland?

A meeting was held and each animal put forth an idea about how to accomplish the task. The Raven was the first to volunteer, but in an attempt to carry fire back from the tree, it singed its feathers. To this day, the Raven remains black. The same was true of both the Racer Snake and the Blacksnake. Each in turn tried and was burned black in its effort to transport the fire. Then the Screech Owl, the Hoot Owl, and the great Horned Owl each took a turn, but they too were unsuccessful. The Screech Owl's eyes are still red from getting too close to the fire, and the Hoot Owl and Great Horned Owl have black rings around their eyes that will not wash off.

When all seemed lost to the animals, the timid Water Spider announced that she might succeed where the others had failed. As the raven, the snakes, and the owls watched, the Water Spider wove a small bowl and attached it to her back. She scampered across the surface of the water to the island, picked up a tiny piece of hot coal from the burning tree, and placed it in the bowl. She then hurried back across the water to the mainland with her precious cargo. And that, according to the Cherokees of long ago, is how fire came to the earth.

Use the Word Bank to fill in the blanks in the sentences below.

> **Word Bank**
>
> black failed sycamore
>
> burning fastened sympathized
>
> cold saved transport

1. In the beginning, all the animals were very _____ .

2. The gods of thunder _____ with the plight of the animals.

3. The gods of thunder made a lightning bolt strike a _____ tree.

4. The _____ tree delighted the animals.

5. The animals discussed ways to _____ the fire from the island to the mainland.

6. Both the Raven and the Racer Snake are _____ because of their efforts to transport the fire.

7. Several owls also _____ to accomplish the task.

8. The Water Spider _____ the day for the animals.

9. The Water Spider carried a hot coal to the mainland in a small bowl it had woven and _____ to its back.

Kertchoo!

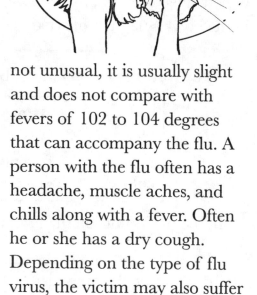

You have a sore throat and a runny nose. You may have a slight fever and even complain of aches in your arms and legs. You tell your parent or guardian that you cannot go to school today because you have the flu.

Or do you? In all probability, unless it is at the height of the flu (influenza) season or unless you are very, very sick, you more likely have a common cold. But how can you tell the difference?

Colds and influenza share certain characteristics. Both are caused by viruses and are transmitted by infected persons spreading droplets of fluid by sneezing or coughing. Both, if not treated properly, can turn into more complicated illnesses like bronchitis and pneumonia. And both usually last from a few days to up to a week and a half.

The flu is a more serious illness than the common cold. Although a fever with a cold is not unusual, it is usually slight and does not compare with fevers of 102 to 104 degrees that can accompany the flu. A person with the flu often has a headache, muscle aches, and chills along with a fever. Often he or she has a dry cough. Depending on the type of flu virus, the victim may also suffer from nausea and vomiting. The flu can leave a person exhausted for weeks after all other symptoms have disappeared.

Colds can occur at almost any time, but the flu breaks out in epidemics. Sometimes these epidemics kill thousands of people. The worst flu epidemic in history occurred in 1918–1919. It swept through Europe and America and claimed 20 million lives. An epidemic that occurs worldwide is called a pandemic.

Persons who are at the greatest risk from an attack of the flu are the very young, the very old, and those who suffer from some other health problem. Fortu-nately, immunizations are available today that provide some measure of protection against these diseases. All persons at high risk are encouraged to take these shots before the onset of cach ycar's flu scason.

Fill in the Venn Diagram with facts about a cold and the flu. List features common to both where the circles overlap.

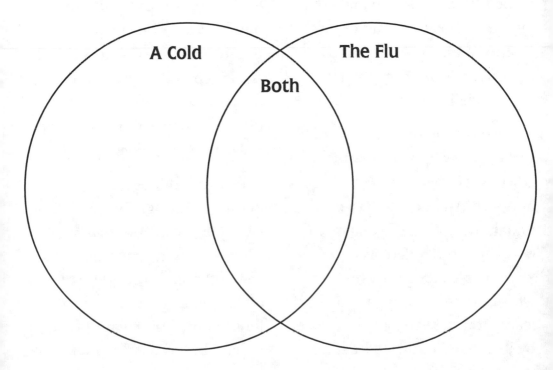

Bill Pickett, Black Cowboy

Old Western movies about cowboys and cattle drives usually picture cowboys as rough-and-ready white men, fearless and as tough as nails. Most, to be sure, were fearless and tough. But not all were white. Many cowboys were Mexican and black.

In the years following the Civil War, many blacks went west to seek their fortunes. Some became homesteaders, while others joined ranch crews and became cowboys. One even became a famous rodeo performer. His name was Bill Pickett.

Born during the Civil War, Bill Pickett grew up and became a cowboy. He worked on ranches in South America, Texas, and Oklahoma. While in Oklahoma, he started the rodeo event known as bulldogging, or steer wrestling. In bulldogging, a rider leaps from a horse, grabs a steer by its horns, and wrestles it to the ground.

Bill Pickett even added a personal twist to the event. Once he had the steer on the ground, he would clamp his strong teeth firmly onto the animal's upper lip. Then, without using his hands or arms, he would cause the steer to flip onto its side. Although bulldogging quickly became popular everywhere, no other cowboy ever tried to copy Bill's lip-biting style.

In 1905, Bill became a member of a touring wild west show. One year, while performing in Mexico City, a group of people were offended by his technique of throwing a steer. They offered him $5,000 if he would enter a bull ring with a ferocious bull. He did not have to try to wrestle the bull to the ground, which would have been impossible, but only to hold on to the beast for five seconds. Smug in their bet, many spectators hoped the bull would gore the black cowboy to death.

A huge crowd turned out to see the spectacle. Even the president of Mexico was in attendance. In a short time, the raging bull gored Bill's horse, forcing the cowboy to jump off and grab his attacker by the horns. Although he received numerous cuts and several broken ribs, Bill held on for the required five seconds and collected his money. Most of the 25,000 people watching the event were highly disappointed.

Bill Pickett later bought a large ranch in Oklahoma and lived to the age of 71.

Number the following events in the life of Bill Pickett in the order that they occured.

Bill Pickett . . .

_____ joined a wild west show.

_____ bought a large ranch in Oklahoma.

_____ became a cowboy.

_____ took on a bull in a Mexico City bull ring.

_____ invented or started bulldogging.

Thinking Cap

What might have motivated Bill Pickett to display such courage and daring as a rodeo performer?

Slaughter at Grant Field

Sometimes a college football team that loses a game by a wide margin accuses the winning eleven of running up the score. Occasionally, the charge is true. Some teams want to score as many points as possible to impress sports writers and coaches.

No year in college produced more lopsided scores than the season of 1916. The University of Tulsa routed Missouri Mines, 117–0; Ohio State smashed Oberlin College, 128–0; and Oklahoma clobbered the Shawnee Catholic Indian School 140–0. But these scores pale compared to what happened to Cumberland College of Lebanon, Tennessee.

In 1916, mighty Georgia Tech was looking for an easy opponent to pad its already impressive record. They found one in tiny Cumberland, which agreed to a game when guaranteed a payment of $500.

Football at Cumberland College was not a priority in 1916. The school, in fact, had no official team. Its coach was a law student who had to search the campus to find sixteen young men willing to play against the Georgia Tech powerhouse. The small squad practiced hard, learned a few simple plays, and boarded a train to Atlanta and a date with destiny.

One thousand spectators bought tickets to watch the game. Georgia Tech scored almost every time it touched the ball. Cumberland had no success on offense and turned the ball over nine times on fumbles. The points mounted so quickly that Cumberland changed its strategy in the first quarter and began to kick off rather than receive after every Georgia Tech score. But no matter what the overmatched squad from Tennessee tried, nothing worked. At the end of the quarter, Georgia Tech led, 63–0. By halftime the score was 126–0. Midway into the third quarter the score had increased to 156–0. When the game mercifully ended, Georgia Tech had won by the incredible score of 222–0!

Write the letter of the correct answer that completes each statement.

_____ 1. Cumberland agreed to a game with Tech because . . .
   a. the players thought it would be a lot of fun.
   b. Cumberland's coach thought his team had a good chance at winning.
   c. the college was offered a sum of money to play.

_____ 2. Cumberland's strategy of kicking off rather than receiving after each Tech score was an attempt to . . .
   a. improve on its kicking game.
   b. hold the score down.
   c. confuse the Tech team.

_____ 3. Georgia Tech scored an equal number of points in the . . .
   a. first and second quarters.
   b. first and third quarters.
   c. second and fourth quarters.

_____ 4. The game was played in . . .
   a. Lebanon, Tennessee.
   b. Atlanta, Georgia.
   c. a site not revealed by the story.

The Armored Animal

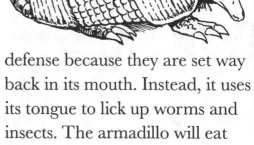

When the Spanish *conquistadores* explored Central America and South America many years ago, they encountered a most strange little animal. It had a small, oblong head with a body and tail covered by hard, bony plates. Like a turtle, the animal's body was completely covered with a hard shell. However, unlike the turtle, its shell did not consist of one piece; instead, it was made up of a number of overlapping plates. The Spanish gave this unusual animal the name armadillo, which means "little armored thing" in Spanish.

The kind of armadillo found in the United States is about two feet long from its head to the tip of its tail. It lives in a burrow, and generally comes out at night to hunt for food. It has strong claws that enable it to dig in grasses and roots for prey as well as to burrow and tunnel in the ground. The armadillo's teeth are useless for biting or self-defense because they are set way back in its mouth. Instead, it uses its tongue to lick up worms and insects. The armadillo will eat almost anything it can catch. Its diet also includes roots and fruits.

The armadillo is unusual in several ways. First, the female gives birth to four babies, and they are always of the same sex. Second, when an armadillo is cornered and cannot escape to its burrow or quickly dig itself into the ground, it rolls itself into a tight, protective ball. This is possible because of the joined overlapping plates of its shell. The armadillo also tucks in its head and feet. If, by chance, it manages to reach the safety of its burrow, the armadillo can hold on so tightly with its strong claws that it is virtually impossible to pull it out.

Yet another way in which the armadillo is unusual is in its ability to float across a river or stream. Using its short but swift legs, it can hurl itself into the water at great speed. Swallowing air makes the animal buoyant, turning its shell into a boat, allowing it to float safely across.

Through the years, the armadillo gradually spread from Central and South America to the United States. It is found in the southcentral and southeastern parts of the country. Because its flesh has a pork-like taste, some people eat it as a delicacy.

Answer the following questions:

1. How did the armadillo get its name? _____

_____

2. What makes it possible for an armadillo to roll its shell into a ball?

_____

3. What do armadillos eat? _____

4. Where is the armadillo found in the United States? _____

_____

5. What is unusual about the babies born to a female armadillo?

_____

6. How is the armadillo able to float? _____

_____

7. Why is the armadillo sometimes eaten as a delicacy?

_____

The Legend of Molly Pitcher

Sometimes feats attributed to famous people are questionable or simply untrue. Such is the case with Molly Pitcher of Revolutionary War fame.

Molly, whose real name was Mary Ludwig, was married to a soldier named John Hays. Hays was a gunner in the First Pennsylvania Artillery which saw action in 1778 at the Battle of Monmouth in New Jersey. When Hays went into battle, Molly went with him. While in camp, she cooked, washed clothes, and did other chores.

On the day the battle was fought, the weather was hot and humid. Molly busied herself carrying pitchers of water to thirsty and wounded American soldiers, and that is how she acquired the name *Molly Pitcher*. That part of her story is true, and her bravery made her a real American heroine. Many years after the conclusion of the war, the Pennsylvania state legislature even awarded her a yearly pension of $40.

What is doubtful about Molly's part in the Battle of Monmouth is the belief by many that she took an active part in the fighting. Legend says that she took over her husband's cannon when he was overcome by the heat of the gun and by the excessive temperature of the day. Another legend maintains that, once the battle was over, Molly received a commission in the army from none other than George Washington himself. Both stories appear to be just that: legends.

But not to worry. There was another Revolutionary War heroine who actually did fire her husband's cannon after he was killed at Fort Washington. Her name was Margaret Corbin. She was severely wounded, and a monument was later erected at West Point in her honor. Why she never received the acclaim granted to Molly Pitcher is a strange twist of history.

Place a check (✓) in the blank to the left of each statement that is **true** of Molly Pitcher.

_____ 1. My real name was Margaret Corbin.

_____ 2. I was married to a soldier.

_____ 3. I followed my husband to camp and into battle.

_____ 4. I am a heroine of the Revolutionary War.

_____ 5. I fought at Fort Washington.

_____ 6. My husband was overcome by heat at the Battle of Monmouth.

_____ 7. I took over and fired my husband's gun.

_____ 8. I carried pitchers of water to soldiers at Monmouth.

_____ 9. I was granted a pension by the state of Pennsylvania.

_____ 10. A monument at West Point was erected in my honor.

_____ 11. I was given an officer's commission by George Washington.

_____ 12. I was wounded at the Battle of Monmouth.

Don't Mess with Mother

They were certainly a noisy and ill-tempered lot. Wherever they went, they created havoc and stirred up the neighborhood. The French called them *chars d'assaut*. The Germans were terrified of them.

Are we talking about the neighbors down the street with a houseful of rowdy children? No. We are referring to the first tanks to appear on the battlefield.

The first tank, or assault vehicle, was built by the British in 1915. It was called Little Willie after the nickname given by the British troops to the son of the German Kaiser, or emperor. Little Willie, however, never made it into battle. Structural defects gave it poor balance, and it was unable to travel across ditches and other obstacles with much success.

The British went back to work and came up with a second tank: Big Willie. It did not have the same balance problem, and it could travel at the breathtaking speed of 3.7 mph. Big Willie eventually came to be called Mother. Subsequent tanks modeled after Mother were called Mother's children. These were the tanks that appeared on the battlefield of Somme in France in 1916.

The British managed to keep the tank secret until its use. When the new machines were being transported by railway or ship, they were covered and labeled "water tanks for Russia." That is how the name "tank" came about.

Forty-nine tanks were sent into action against the Germans.

Only eighteen actually engaged the enemy; the others either broke down or got stuck in mud. But these few proved effective.

How did the Germans react when they first saw these giant, snail-like monstrosities lumbering toward their trenches? Many pointed and roared with laughter. Others screamed. But they all reacted in the same way when "Mother's children" started spitting fire in their direction. They quickly fled to the rear!

The meaning of a word sometimes depends on the way it is used in a sentence. Use the Word Bank to fill in the blanks below.

The tank was _____ to the battlefield by the British in Word War I. When it _____ at the Somme in 1916, it _____ the Germans.

An earlier tank used by the British _____ ineffective. It got _____ in ditches and had a _____ to overturn. Its _____ , called Big Willie, was _____ reliable. And it could _____ a speed of almost 4 mph!

Big Willie was a _____ machine that _____ a big, metal box. But it _____ its purpose. When the Germans first saw it, they _____ in amazement. Many thought the _____ was funny. Then it began to _____ fire. At that, the Germans turned and fled.

Word Bank				
appeared	cumbersome	introduced	proved	resembled
attain	fulfilled	monstrosity	stuck	tendency
belch	gazed	more	successor	terrified

Mammal, Fish, or Fowl?

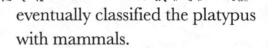

When scientists in England received reports from Australia about the duckbill platypus in the late 1700s, they thought they were the victims of a hoax. Surely, they must have reasoned, some jokester had sewn body parts from several different animals together in an attempt to trick them.

Indeed, the duckbill platypus is a strange animal. It has a bill resembling a duck, a flat, paddle-shaped tail like a beaver, and it scuffles along on the ground in the manner of an alligator. Both its front and hind feet are webbed and have claws. Unlike most mammals, it has neither lips nor exterior ears. Although it nurses its young, it does not give birth to live babies. Instead, it lays eggs—like a chicken! Small wonder that scientists were confused and not certain whether they were dealing with fish, fowl, or some kind of new species. They eventually classified the platypus with mammals.

The platypus uses its bill to nuzzle in mud, searching for worms, grubs, and shellfish. It is protected while in the water by its thick, grayish-brown fur. In size, the platypus measures up to two feet in length including its tail of 4 to 5 inches. The male is slightly larger than the female and has poisonous spurs on the ankle of each leg. Like a viper, the male uses these spurs to inject poison into an attacker.

The female platypus lays no more than two or three eggs at a time. When the babies hatch and begin to grow, they are fed in a most unusual way. The mother does not have nipples like other mammals, but its underside has pores through which milk seeps. As she lies on her back, milk oozes from the pores for her babies to lap up.

The platypus is native only to Australia and Tasmania. Because it was once hunted almost to extinction for its fur, it is today under the protection of the Australian government.

Write the letter of the correct answer to each statement.

_____ 1. The duckbill platypus is native only to . . .
    a. Tasmania.
    b. Australia.
    c. both of the above.

_____ 2. Poisonous spurs are located on the hind legs of the . . .
    a. male platypus.
    b. female platypus.
    c. both.

_____ 3. The female platypus lays . . .
    a. only one egg at a time.
    b. no more than two to three eggs at a time.
    c. up to five eggs at a time.

_____ 4. When a platypus moves around, it resembles a (an) . . .
    a. badger.
    b. duck.
    c. alligator.

_____ 5. The diet of the platypus consists of . . .
    a. worms, grubs, and shellfish.
    b. fruits and berries.
    c. small rodents.

Tall-Tale Titan: Pecos Bill

Lumberjacks had Paul Bunyan. African-Americans sang the praises of John Henry. And cowboys of the wild west had Pecos Bill.

Pecos Bill was a legendary super-cowboy born in eastern Texas in the 1830s. He was raised by coyotes, and for many years he thought he was one. Bill grew up in the wilds after bouncing off a wagon while traveling west with his family. He fell near the Pecos River in west Texas and was never missed by his parents. They had so many children that Bill's absence was not noticed until it was too late to turn back.

Cowboys of the Pecos River region were a rough and fearsome lot. It was only natural that they would invent a character like Pecos Bill. Among his exploits, Bill ended a long drought in Texas by digging the Rio Grande River to get water from the Gulf of Mexico. On another occasion, he rode a cyclone without a saddle until it "rained out" from under him. The resulting downpour created the Grand Canyon. Bill was also credited with inventing roping and other skills important to cowboys. After becoming a cowboy, he rode a wild horse named Widow Maker.

Bill is most famous for riding a mountain lion into the camp of a particularly tough trail outfit, using a 12-foot rattlesnake as a lasso. He had tamed both animals after "whipping" them in a fist fight. After arriving at his destination, he asked the terrified cowboys who their boss was. Immediately, a 7-foot giant of a man looked at Bill and replied, "Well, I was, but *you* are now!"

Many stories exist as to how Pecos Bill died. Perhaps one of the most interesting is that he washed down a meal of barbed wire with nitroglycerin.

Number the events below about Pecos Bill in the order that they appear in the story.

Pecos Bill . . .

_____ became boss of a trail outfit.

_____ fell near the Pecos River.

_____ tamed a mountain lion and a rattlesnake.

_____ bounced off a wagon while on his way west.

_____ dug the Rio Grande River.

_____ grew up with coyotes.

_____ took a ride on a cyclone.

Write meanings for the following words from the story. You may use a dictionary if necessary.

1. fearsome _____

2. drought _____

3. cyclone _____

4. destination _____

5. exploits _____

A Terrible Dilemma

During your lifetime, you will have to make many decisions. Some will be very difficult. Even today, you must make decisions that affect your life and the lives of those around you. Whatever the circumstances, decisions often are not easy. Sometimes you leave yourself open to criticism regardless of what you decide to do.

President Harry Truman was faced with such a situation in the summer of 1945. World War II in Europe had ended, and the United States and its allies were trying to bring the war against Japan to a successful conclusion. The Japanese were all but defeated, but their military leaders stubbornly refused to surrender. President Truman and his advisers realized that stronger measures were necessary to end the war.

The President had two choices. One was to approve an invasion of the Japanese home-land. The other was to authorize use of a terrible new weapon that the United States had tested in New Mexico a few weeks earlier. That weapon was the world's first atomic bomb.

As for the first choice, experts estimated that a land invasion of Japan would cause over two million deaths. And the war would drag on. The second choice would also have terrible consequences. Thousands of innocent civilians, including women and children, would be killed. Many others would die from the effects of radiation. No one knew for certain what the overall destructive force of the atomic bomb would be.

After listening to advisers and pondering the possible results of both choices, the President decided to use the atomic bomb. Although many people would die and it would cause terrible destruction, the President felt it would shorten the war and save millions of lives.

In early August 1945, atomic bombs were dropped on the Japanese cities of Hiroshima and Nagasaki. More than 120,000 people were killed. On August 14, Japan surrendered, and World War II was over.

Write your opinions to the questions below.

1. Was President Truman right or wrong in using the atomic bomb against Japan? Give reasons why you feel the way you do.

_____

_____

_____

2. Do you think Japan's military leaders were responsible for the catastrophe that happened to their country? Why or why not?

_____

_____

_____

3. Explain what effect the A-bomb would have on future warfare.

_____

_____

_____

Tiny Tom

As a young boy, Charles Stratton was only 25 inches tall and weighed but 15 pounds. But he used his small size to advantage and became one of the world's best-known show persons.

Stratton was a midget born to normal-sized parents in 1838. Because of a pituitary gland that did not function properly, he remained very tiny. When he was four, his parents permitted him to join the New York City museum operated by Phineas T. Barnum, a showman and later circus owner. Barnum's museum displayed giants, dwarfs, and other oddities, as well as a number of hoaxes which people took to be genuine. One was an exhibit called the "Feejee Mermaid," which turned out to be a monkey and a fish sewn together. Another was an 80-year-old woman whom Barnum passed off as the 161-year-old nurse of George Washington. Because of these hoaxes, some people referred to Barnum as the "Prince of Humbug." But Stratton, to whom Barnum gave the stage name General Tom Thumb, was very real. And he made a lot of money for himself and his employer.

When P.T. Barnum took his museum on tour, Thumb would entertain show-goers by singing and dancing. Barnum took him to Europe several times, where he met England's Queen Victoria and other royalty. Everywhere he went, Thumb was a sensation. After Barnum got out of the museum business, the famous showman started a traveling circus known as *The Greatest Show on Earth*. Once again, General Tom Thumb was a star attraction.

Thumb eventually grew to be 40 inches tall and weighed 70 pounds. But he was still very small compared to someone of normal height. In 1863, he married Lavinia Warren, a midget who was also a member of Barnum's traveling museum.

During his years with the museum and the circus, Thumb spent money almost as fast as he earned it. When he died at the age of 45, he had nothing left, although he had once been a wealthy man.

Using words from the story, fill in the blanks in the sentences below to complete the puzzle about Tom Thumb.

1. Tom Thumb weighed _____ pounds as a young boy.

2. Charles _____ was Tom Thumb's real name.

3. In size, Tom Thumb was a _____ .

4. Tom was a performer with *The Greatest Show on* _____ .

5. The Feejee Mermaid was a _____ .

6. Tom Thumb toured _____ on several occasions.

7. Phineas T. _____ was Tom Thumb's employer.

8. The "Prince of _____" probably fooled many people in his lifetime.

Thinking Cap

Why do you think Charles Stratton's parents allowed him to join Phineas T. Barnum's museum at the tender age of four?

Butchery on the Plains

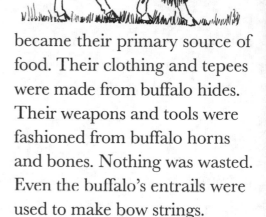

Until the latter part of the nineteenth century, millions of buffalo roamed the prairie lands of the Great Plains. These mighty animals, more correctly known as American bison, were literally the source of life for the Plains Indians. But in the years following the Civil War, white buffalo hunters rushed to the area and slaughtered most of the great herds. In so doing, they did more than almost wipe out a majestic animal. They destroyed a way of life that had existed for hundreds of years.

Native Americans did not kill the buffalo for sport or profit as the white man did. Instead, they believed the buffalo was a gift from the Great Spirit, and they only killed it when necessary to obtain food and other essentials. And, unlike the white hunters who took the hides and left the meat to rot on the prairie, the Indians used every part of the animal. The buffalo's flesh became their primary source of food. Their clothing and tepees were made from buffalo hides. Their weapons and tools were fashioned from buffalo horns and bones. Nothing was wasted. Even the buffalo's entrails were used to make bow strings.

Sometimes buffalo hunters and sportsmen shot several hundred animals a day. Often this was done from trains that stopped on the prairie for the sole purpose of allowing a sportsman to record a kill. Hunters alone were responsible for shipping 1,250,000 hides back east by rail in 1873. Ten years later, most of the herds were gone, and the Plains Indians were reduced to eating coyotes and dogs. Some sources say that only about 540 buffalo were left in the U.S. in 1882.

But the Indians could not look to the U.S. government for help. The army supported the buffalo's destruction, for without the buffalo, the Plains Indians would be reduced to starvation and thereby easy to subdue. That is exactly what happened in 1890, only a short time after the great herds had been killed off.

In time, the government realized measures had to be taken to protect the few remaining buffalo. Laws were passed making it illegal to hunt and kill the animals. Thus, the wild buffalo was saved from extinction. Unfortunately, it was too late to preserve the traditional lifestyle of the Plains Indians.

Match the year to the event by writing the correct letter in the blank to the left of each statement.

A. 1883 C. 1873
B. 1890 D. 1882

_____ 1. year by which most of the buffalo had disappeared.

_____ 2. year in which only about 540 buffalo remained in the United States.

_____ 3. year 1,250,000 hides were shipped east.

_____ 4. year in which resistance on the part of the Plains Indians ended.

Thinking Cap

Explain the position of the government toward the slaughter of the buffalo. _____

_____

Pouch Potatoes

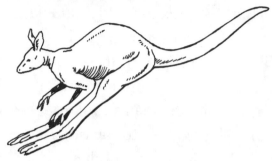

You are no doubt familiar with the slang term "couch potato," referring to someone whose leisure time is devoted to lying around and watching TV.

Making use of a play on words, we might call the young of certain mammals "pouch potatoes." These are the babies of marsupials, a class of mammals having a pouch. The pouch is a fold of skin under the abdomen of the mother marsupial. Here the undeveloped babies nurse and live during the first several months of their lives. Even after a baby is quite large, it will often retreat to the safety of its mother's pouch when threatened.

Nearly all marsupials today live in Australia. Only one, the opossum, is native to North America. Marsupials thrive in many kinds of environments; some live in trees while others live on the ground or in burrows. They range in size from small, pouched Australian mice and moles to the majestic red kangaroo. The latter is the largest of all marsupials. It stands about six feet tall and can weigh up to 200 pounds. Its long hind legs enables it to leap or bounce along the ground at speeds of more than 30 miles an hour.

Besides the small rodents and the red kangaroo in size, there are a number of other interesting marsupials. Two are the wallaby, a smaller type of kangaroo, and the koala, which resembles a bear and eats only eucalyptus leaves.

The most unusual marsupial is the now almost extinct

Tasmanian wolf. It differs from other marsupials in that its pouch opens to the back instead of the front of its body. It has not been spotted in the wilds for almost 70 years.

Yet another marsupial native to Tasmania is the Tasmanian devil. Cartoons have pictured the devil as a savage beast that eats almost anything. In general, this is true, although devils hunt small animals and often eat the remains of dead animals.

On the blank line to the left of each sentence, write **T** if the statement is true or **F** if it is false.

_____ 1. Marsupials live only on the ground.

_____ 2. The koala's diet consists solely of the leaves of the eucalyptus tree.

_____ 3. The largest marsupial is the red kangaroo.

_____ 4. The Tasmanian devil subsists chiefly on a diet of insects.

_____ 5. The wallaby is a kind of wolf.

_____ 6. Most marsupials live in Australia.

_____ 7. The Tasmanian wolf has increased in numbers so much that it is a threat to farmers.

_____ 8. The koala is a true bear.

_____ 9. Red kangaroos stand as tall as most men.

_____ 10. The opossum is the smallest of the marsupials.

Early "Rock"

When you hear the term "rock music," you may think of such rock forms as rap, heavy metal, country, surf, disco, or punk. Each at one time attained some degree of popularity in the United States, and several remain popular today. And you probably think of such performers as Bruce Springsteen, the Rolling Stones, Madonna, the Jefferson Airplane, the Smashing Pumpkins, and others.

But rock music from the 1970s to the present bears little resemblance to that of the 1950s, when rock began. Originally known as rock 'n' roll, it was the first music that American teenagers could claim as their own. Its themes were centered around dances, cars, and boy/girl relationships. And it was simple: rock 'n' roll music generally used only two or three chords that were easy to remember.

The first rock band of note in the 1950s was Bill Haley and the Comets. Their recording of "Rock Around the Clock" is still played on radio stations today. The first rock superstar, of course, was Elvis Presley. His first big hit was "Heartbreak Hotel" in 1956. Another early rock star was Chuck Berry, who recorded "Maybellene" in 1955.

Rock 'n' roll lost some of its appeal toward the end of the 1950s. Elvis Presley was drafted into the army, and scandals plagued several other leading artists. But it saw a quick revival with the appearance of the Beatles, a rock group from England. The Beatles made rock 'n' roll popular throughout the world. They added their own brand of sophistication and wit to the music. Even older listeners were attracted to their music. It wasn't until later in the sixties that rock groups began to base many of their songs on social and political issues.

Write the letter of the correct answer in the blank to the left of each question.

_____ 1. Rock's first superstar was . . .
  a. Elvis Presley.
  b. Bill Haley.
  c. Bruce Springsteen.

_____ 2. Near the end of the 1950s, rock 'n' roll . . .
  a. became more popular than ever.
  b. spread internationally.
  c. experienced a temporary decline.

_____ 3. The first important rock band of the 1950s was . . .
  a. the Jefferson Airplane.
  b. Bill Haley and the Comets.
  c. the Rolling Stones.

_____ 4. The following is true of rock 'n' roll music of the 1950s.
  a. Young people claimed it as their own.
  b. It was simple, with easy melodies and just a few chords.
  c. Both "a" and "b" are true.

_____ 5. The song "Maybellene" was recorded by . . .
  a. Elvis Presley.
  b. Madonna.
  c. Chuck Berry.

_____ 6. The first big international rock group was . . .
  a. the Beatles.
  b. the Rolling Stones.
  c. the Bee Gees.

A Frontier Roughneck

Not all true-to-life American folk characters were heroes, to be admired and looked up to. Some were scoundrels who lived only to drink and fight. But they are interesting because they give us a picture of what life was like in the early days of our country.

One such person was Mike Fink. Mike was a rough-and-ready boatman who worked on keelboats on the Ohio and Mississippi Rivers in the 1800s. He loved fighting and he enjoyed pranks. He once even set his wife Peg's hair and clothing on fire because she was "winkin' at them fellers . . . " A quick dive into the river saved Mrs. Fink from serious injury.

When steamboats appeared and made keelboats obsolete, Mike Fink went west. He joined the Rocky Mountain Fur Company and worked as a boatman and trapper. Always a bully and

a braggart, he challenged another trapper to an unusual contest that indirectly resulted in his death.

Mike Fink bragged that he could outfight and outshoot any man around. He boasted that he was "half-horse, half-alligator, and half-snapping turtle." In 1822, he engaged in a duel with a man named Carpenter. The two took turns shooting a cup of whiskey off each other's head. One of Carpenter's shots grazed Mike, making him more than a little angry. On his next opportunity, Mike shot his adversary through the middle of the forehead. Later, to get even, one of Carpenter's friends shot and killed Mike at point-blank range.

Again, folklore characters like Mike Fink tells us much about our country's early history. Hard work, boasting, tall tales, and brawls were typical of everyday life on the frontier.

Such characters, however, are not good role models for young people. Their kind often came to the same violent end as did Mike Fink.

The following statements refer to the story of Mike Fink. On the line to the left of each sentence, mark **F** if you think the statement is a fact, or **O** if you consider it an opinion.

_____ 1. Mike Fink was the strongest man on the frontier.

_____ 2. Mike Fink moved west when the steamboat came into use.

_____ 3. Everybody on the frontier respected Mike Fink.

_____ 4. Mrs. Peg Fink was afraid of her husband.

_____ 5. Mike Fink liked to brag and fight.

_____ 6. Carpenter's friend was justified in killing Mike Fink.

_____ 7. Stories such as that of Mike Fink tell us much about early frontier people.

_____ 8. Mike Fink is not a good role model for young people to follow.

_____ 9. Fighting and the telling of tall tales were characteristic of frontier people.

Draw a sketch. Find a picture of a keelboat in an encyclopedia or some other source and draw a sketch of it on another sheet of paper.

Ow, Ugh, and Oink

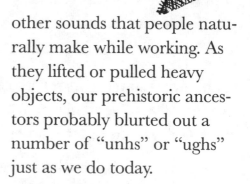

Have you ever wondered how language began? People, to be sure, did not start off saying clever things like "Good morning" or "How do you do?" or "You're grounded for the next three weeks!" Nor did they sit down first thing and write out an alphabet. Somewhere, at some point, sounds were adopted that represented thoughts and ideas.

There are many theories or ideas about how language started. A favorite of some philologists—people who study the origin of language— is the "pooh-pooh" theory. This idea states that language began as exclamations of pain, surprise, pleasure, and other emotions. Thus, cries like "ow," "oh," and "aahh" may have been some of humankind's first words.

Closely related to the "pooh-pooh" theory is the "yo-he-ho" theory. It holds that language sprang from the grunts and other sounds that people naturally make while working. As they lifted or pulled heavy objects, our prehistoric ancestors probably blurted out a number of "unhs" or "ughs" just as we do today.

A third theory about language development is the "bow-wow" theory. It is based on the belief that language resulted from people imitating the sounds made by animals. Did everyone go around barking, bleating, and roaring? Probably not. They may have simply named animals by the sounds they made. If so, when the dog first appeared and barked, our ancestors might have labeled it an "arf." Likewise, a cow might have been called a "moo" and a pig an "oink." Who knows? One person's thoughts about how language started are just as valid as another's.

But one thing is certain: humankind had a spoken language thousands of years before anything was put down in writing. The earliest known word-pictures were those of the Sumarians, dating from about 3500 B.C. The most popular picture writing—hieroglyphics—was used by the ancient Egyptians. It remained for the Phoenicians of northern Africa to later change these pictures into what became our alphabet.

Complete the following.

1. Tell which one of the three theories about how language began is the most logical, and why. Then tell about any ideas of your own that may differ from these established theories.

_____

_____

_____

_____

_____

_____

2. Imagine yourself marooned on an island with five other people. Because each of you speaks a different language, no one can understand a word the others are saying. How might your group learn to communicate? Write a short essay on another sheet of paper.

Upstaging the Führer

You have probably heard of Adolf Hitler, the dictator of Nazi Germany. He and his Nazi Party ruled that country with an iron hand from 1933 to 1945. After World War II began in 1939, his armies conquered most of Europe. Everywhere the Nazis went, they spread terror and fear. During their twelve years in power, they were responsible for the deaths of millions of Jews and other peoples the Germans considered "inferior."

Hitler and the Nazis believed that the Germans were a "master race," destined to rule the world. And since they considered themselves superior to other people, they reasoned that their superiority would give them an edge in all endeavors, including athletics. Were they ever surprised at the Olympic Games that were held in Berlin in the summer of 1936!

Hitler expected Germany's athletes to outshine those from other nations, especially black athletes. Little did he realize that Jesse Owens of the United States would completely shatter these far-fetched theories.

Owens, a black American, won four gold medals, thereby establishing himself as one of the greatest track and field stars of all time. He won the 100-meter dash, the 200-meter dash, and set a new Olympic record for the broad jump. Owens won his fourth gold medal as a member of the U.S. 400-meter relay team.

Hitler was so angry at this unexpected turn of events that he left the Olympic stadium and refused to watch as Owens received his medals.

Jesse Owens returned to America to a ticker-tape parade in New York City. Adolf Hitler returned to his quarters to brood and to try to explain away the triumphs of America's magnificent black athlete.

Choose a synonym from the Word Bank for each vocabulary word below taken from the story and write it on the line on the right. On the line to the left, write how the word is used in the story.

Parts of Speech   Synonyms

_____ 1. destined   _____

_____ 2. superior   _____

_____ 3. endeavors   _____

_____ 4. far-fetched _____

_____ 5. brood   _____

_____ 6. edge   _____

_____ 7. shatter   _____

_____ 8. parade   _____

_____ 9. outshine   _____

_____ 10. conquered _____

Word Bank

advantage	motorcade	undertaking	illogical
fated	better	destroy	upstage
	overrun	mope	

Becoming a Better Reader

There are a number of ways in which you can improve your reading skills and become a better reader. Here are some suggestions.

- **Avoid materials too far below your reading level.** Challenge yourself. Try reading something that may be a grade level higher than what you are accustomed to reading. But be careful; don't try to read material that is *too* difficult.

- **Look up unfamiliar words in a dictionary.** You cannot fully understand any passage you read if you skim over unfamiliar words. Look them up!

- **Watch for context clues.** Often the words preceding and coming after a word will give you a clue to its meaning.

- **Become familiar with prefixes and suffixes.** Prefixes such as "re," "pre," and "un," and suffixes such as "er," "ing," and "ment" are added to base or root words to form many other words. Knowing prefixes and suffixes will increase your reading vocabulary many times over.

- **Ask for help.** Ask your teacher, parent or guardian, or a friend to explain a word or phrase in a passage you do not understand. Don't be shy. Ask for help.